What's cooking?

Last Minute Cuisine

QUICK MEALS

www.apollo-intermedia.de

Complete production: Naumann & Göbel Verlagsgesellschaft mbH, Cologne
Printed in Germany

ISBN 3-625-10932-8

What's cooking?

Last Minute Cuisine

QUICK MEALS

NAUMANN & GÖBEL

Contents

Last-Minute-Cuisine

Do not let your lack of time take away the pleasure of eating! You will be amazed at how quick, how healthy and especially how ingenious the recipes are. It will only take you half an hour at the most to produce even the tastiest meals. Our tips for keeping a well-stocked kitchen and for those hurried moments as well as the cream of our last-minute-recipes will guide you.

But We Haven't Got the Time!

Quick
It is gone past six and you have not even done your shopping yet! You leave work, rush off to the supermarket. Three good friends of yours are coming round for dinner, you even promised them something special, but have only got one and a half hours to accomplish your mission impossible. Time is snapping at your heels and if you do not get a move on, the door bell will ring while you are unpacking your shopping! How on earth should you go about avoiding dishing up a frozen pizza, tinned ravioli or fish and chips from the local chippy?

Healthy
You have got one hour before you need to pick up your eldest son, your little girl has to go to the doctor's – she has been giving you an earful because of stomach cramps. And do not forget to pick up the smallest one from the kindergarten! As luck would have it, his kindergarten teacher wants to have a word with you, too. And your piano student will want to show you all she has learned... Call that a full programme! How are you supposed to squeeze in the shopping? Especially as you are tired and worn out? So what can you dish up for the family tonight? Fish fingers or Heinz spaghetti? Normally you always try to produce healthy and fresh food full of vitamins. Is it really not possible to stop off at the local greengrocers and produce something edible tonight?

Ingenious
Things got a bit out of hand last night. Good thing that nothing much is on today. You have missed the lectures anyway and can take it easy for the rest of the day. Have you forgotten anything? ... Oh, yes, Catherine! Of course! She is coming over tonight. That spoiled little girl you fancy... Well, the day is not totally lost then! But you promised her culinary delights. What to do now? Especially since the hangover from last night has you firmly in its grip. There is no chance of becoming a chef in that mood! Is it possible to dish something up that is both simple and yet ingenious? One thing is for certain: You must not disgrace yourself. Not in front of Catherine!

Time – the one thing that only very few have too much of. The pace of life is increasing, a fact that is reflected in each step of our everyday existence. We rush from day to day through our jobs, our leisure time, our whole lives. Even the little time left to us that we can call our own develops quickly and quite unconsciously into something that we have got to rush through. We do not want to miss out on anything. We want to experience all there is to experience and get an impression of everything. In eighty days around the world is old hat – one day will have to do, we have not got the time any more. No wonder then that we are rushed off our feet when it comes to eating. But this is one area where we should not be stingy and should not be bothered about the odd minute or two. In France they still know what it means to devote oneself to the pleasures that eating can afford. There they take all the time in the world to properly enjoy their food. And a touch of that Southern lifestyle would do wonders in our fast-food-culture. Instead of stuffing down that hamburger from the drive-in on your way to work, instead of slurping the soup directly from the tin as you walk out of the front door, instead of making space for a bag of chips before you rush off to the cinema – instead of all this – we should calm down, take things slowly and sit down at the table, be it with the family, just the two of you, with friends or all on your own. You should take time out for this because this way of taking stock is healthy and pleasant, serves to reduce stress and increases your inner calmness. Nevertheless, all that is easier said than done. Of course, you simply have not got the time! However, all you need to do is play a couple of tricks on your busy schedule by spending as little time as possible on preparation and as much time as possible on the event itself, namely eating. You will be amazed at how quick, how healthy and especially how ingenious the following recipes are. Get cooking now and you will produce the tastiest dishes in less than 30 minutes.

You will gain a new attitude towards the kitchen and cooking that will make your evenings less stressful. Instead you will start to enjoy spending time with family and friends again. Last-minute cuisine, last-minute-cooking, one hundred percent enjoyment!

Preparation

Last-minute cuisine means dishing up delicious food at the last minute without stress. You do not have to be an experienced chef or impassioned cooking geek. Much more important for the last-minute cuisine is good organisation. This means that if you do not find the time to go shopping you will be able to use what there is at home. A well thought through larder full of different foods, partly non-perishable, partly convenience products is the solution.

Last Minute Out of the Can

Do not shy away from frozen or preserved foods! The quality of these products is surprisingly good nowadays. However, people still cannot quite believe it. You should bear in mind though that with the raw product processed straight away, we can take it for granted that the quality is excellent. One should also be aware that this method eliminates long transportation times of the product in its fresh state – and this is when it loses most of its vitamins.

Moreover, controlled growing conditions guarantee consistently high quality. Storable foods also have very good nutritional values as they are processed with exactly that in mind.

What cans, jars, bottles and frozen foods should you always have at your disposal then?

One thing that you should never be without is tinned **tomatoes** to make delicious sauces, dips and pizza toppings. While their fresh counterparts require more time to peel (first put them in hot water, rinse with cold water, then peel), all you need for the canned variety is a can-opener.

Peas, beans and lentils should always find a place in your larder. Tinned pulses are ideal for quick salads, stews and pastes. On the one hand you save yourself the long soaking times and on the other you do not have to compromise on quality. Frozen peas are also excellent. They do not lack taste compared to their fresh counterparts and vitamins, nutritional value, appearance and colour remain unchanged from the time of picking. The same goes for **spinach** and **kale**. Again, you should really always have a packet of either of them in your freezer.

Canned **tuna** and **anchovies** in oil improve any salad or sauce. If you have got these ingredients in your cupboard you approach gourmet level! **Gherkins**, **capers** and **olives** you should not be without either.

Sauerkraut and **red cabbage** preserved in either glass or can are welcome side dishes for a spontaneous Sunday roast. All you need is an apple or some well chosen spices and nobody will suspect that they are eating preserved stuff.

Canned **sweetcorn** and **red kidney beans** are quite simply a must for all lovers of colourful salads and Mexican food. How would you make an authentic chilli-con-carne without them?

Last Minute Basics

Apart from tins, cans and jars – all of which you can stack neatly in the cupboard – there are a few more provisions you would not want to do without. Again, you should make sure the following are regulars in your kitchen: for example, you will need **spices** and **dried herbs** all the time. You will revolutionise more than one dish simply by adding the right classy aroma. With so little doing so much, you should always make sure you have salt and pepper, cayenne pepper, curry, cumin, cardamom, cinnamon and rosemary, oregano and thyme handy. **Mustard, Tabasco sauce, Worcester sauce** and other spicy sauces are also absolute essentials which add a certain touch to your dishes. Also, you will never be in a tight spot when it comes to flavour. **Stock cubes** round off your selection of the spice section.

Onions, **garlic** and **potatoes** are **classics** you always need to have at your disposal. Store them in a dry, cool place and they stay fresh for some three weeks, ready to save you in your hour of need! **Oil** and **vinegar** should of course never be amiss either.

"Basics" in the true sense of the word are **pasta**, **rice**, **sugar** and **flour**. Always check the "best before" date and watch out for correct storage conditions. Nearly everything that is not from the freezer is best stored in a dark and dry place. Also make sure it is not too warm. The best way of keeping such foods is to use re-sealable containers.

Frozen Last Minute

The freezer compartment in your fridge - or your chest freezer, if you are fortunate enough to have one, - turns into a prime provider of ingredients in the last-minute kitchen. It should not only contain **chips, peas**, **spinach** and **frozen fish**, but also less basic foods such as **puff pastry**, **prawns** and **frozen fruit**. These will help you to increase your scope of recipes by miles.

And just in case you do not have a vegetable patch which provides you with **fresh herbs** on a daily basis you should simply freeze them: wash, chop and put them in small airtight bags. Now you can prepare top salads even in winter.

Home made meals deserve to find a place in your freezer, too. Properly packaged they will last up to six months. The best thing is that it tastes just as good as when you first made it – all you need to do is heat it up. By the way: do not forget the simplest of them all, **ice cubes**. They always come in handy for a spontaneous cocktail evening...

Last Minute Shopping

Instead of the usual routine of forcing yourself to go round the supermarket every evening it makes sense to designate one day a week for a grand shopping adventure. You use it to close the gaps created by the previous week's cooking and to stock up on food for the coming seven days. Do not buy things off the cuff though, try to be systematic about it. A sort of weekly menu will surely help you with this. Do not worry, we are not asking you to plan day for day in detail. Or worse, work out all your ingredients needed. We are merely talking about a rough plan that gives you an idea of what and how much of something you might need.

Products such as **butter**, **milk**, **eggs**, **fruit** and **vegetables** definitely belong in your weekly shopping trolley – after all, they taste best when they are fresh. When buying butter, milk and other **dairy products** you should always check the "best before" date and plan replenishments when necessary. Fruit and vegetables keep for up to a week in the proper compartment of the refrigerator (note though that lettuce, mushrooms, radish and spinach only last two days). Freshness also plays an important factor when it comes to meat and **bread**. However, if you simply do not have the time to go and get those things fresh, the freezer will do the trick (meat keeps from six to twelve months, bread from one to three months).

To put it in a nutshell, the following pages are ideal for people with little time. They list last-minute-recipes for four people which you will be able to prepare and dish up in no time at all. This means that they are **quick**. It will not take you longer than fifteen, twenty or thirty minutes at the most to cook **healthy** and **ingenious** food for yourself, your friends and family. And all without arduous hour-long preparations, mile-long queues in the supermarket or standing in front of the oven all hot and bothered...
Right then... Let's get cooking!

Salads and Cold Starters

They are really worth the time! Salads and small starters have a few things going for them: not only do they serve as tasty appetizers but you can also prepare them in a jiffy. Just the right thing to get people in the mood. On the following pages you will find the right salad for every taste. The ideal way to start a relaxing evening.

Beetroot Salad

1 lb (500 g) cooked beetroot

2 shallots

3 tbsp olive oil

5 oz (150 g) chopped almonds

1 tbsp lemon juice

1 1/2 tbsp red wine vinegar

sugar

salt

1 firm pear

7 oz (200 g) rocket salad

Preparation time: approx. 20 minutes
Per serving: approx. 367 cals/1542 kj

1 Drain the beetroot using a colander. Then slice the beetroot. Peel and chop the shallots finely.

2 Heat the oil in a frying pan and roast the almonds. Add the shallots and beetroot. Season with the lemon juice, red wine vinegar, sugar, 1 pinch of salt.

3 Peel the pear, cut it in half and core. Then slice the pear into thin slices.

4 Wash and dry the rocket salad. Arrange on four side plates. Place the beetroot and pear slices on top and serve.

In order to prevent the bee-root
(not only a nervine tonic but also hemopoietic)
from discolouring your sclad
you can toss it in oil before cooking.

Crayfish with Aioli

13 oz (400 g) crayfish meat

2 cloves of garlic

1 tbsp coarse salt

1/2 pint (200 ml) of extra virgin olive oil

2 egg yolks

lemon segments for decoration

Preparation time: approx. 10 minutes
Per serving: approx. 460 cals/1933 kj

1 To make the aioli, crush the garlic and beat it together with the egg yolks and salt. Add the olive oil drop by drop until the mixture becomes creamy.

2 Arrange the crayfish meat on plates and add the Aioli. Quarter the lemon and cut the pieces into two. Garnish with the lemon segments and some herbs. A fresh French stick goes nicely with this dish.

Three Vinegar Salad

1 tbsp grainy mustard

1 tbsp red wine vinegar

1 tbsp balsamico vinegar

1 tbsp raspberry vinegar

3 tbsp olive oil

salt

freshly milled pepper

8 lettuce hearts

1 small head of radicchio

8 cooked quail's eggs out of the glass

Preparation time: approx. 10 minutes
Per serving: approx. 145 cals/612 kj

1 Mix the mustard with the olive oil and different vinegars in a bowl. Season with salt and freshly milled pepper.

2 Wash and dry the lettuce hearts and radicchio. Drain the quail's eggs, peel and halve them.

3 Put two lettuce hearts on each side plate. Arrange radicchio and quail's eggs on top and add the salad dressing.

Bean Fish Bowl

1/2 lb (250 g) red kidney bean (tinned)

1 red onion

1/2 cucumber

2 vine-ripened tomatoes

1 tbsp capers

7 oz (200 g) tuna (tinned)

3 tablespoons sherry vinegar

2 tbsp garlic oil

salt

pepper

2 oz (50 g) lamb's lettuce

Preparation time: approx. 25 minutes
Per serving: approx. 390 cals/1639 kj

1 Drain the red kidney beans using a colander. Peel the onion and cut into rings. Wash the cucumber and halve lengthwise. Deseed with a spoon and slice the cucumber.

2 Wash and dry the tomatoes. Halve them, remove the green bits around the stem and slice the tomatoes. Drain the capers and the tuna.

3 Mix the sherry vinegar and garlic oil and season with salt and pepper. Wash the lamb's lettuce. Transfer the lamb's lettuce, beans, onions, cucumber, tomatoes, capers and tuna into a bowl.

4 Pour over the salad dressing and leave to steep for approximately 5 minutes. Arrange on plates and serve.

Try this salad with spotted rosecoco beans either out of a tin or a packet.

Tequila Rice Platter

7 oz (200 g) five-minute rice

salt

3 1/2 oz (100 g) tomato purée

2 tbsp pesto

1 tbsp chilli sauce

1 shot Tabasco sauce

7 oz (200 g) tinned sweetcorn

pepper

7 oz (200 g) cooked shrimps

1 fl oz (3 cl) Tequila

Preparation time: approx. 25 minutes
Per serving: approx. 422 cals/1774 kj

1 Cook the rice following the instructions on the packet in slightly salted water. Mix together the tomato purée, pesto and chilli sauce and add a shot of Tabasco sauce.

2 Drain the sweetcorn using a colander. Add to the mixture. Season everything with salt and pepper.

3 Pour the tequila over the shrimps and leave to soak while the rice is cooling. Then mix the rice, tomato mixture and shrimps together. Arrange on plates and serve.

Smoked Fish Salad "Neptune"

8 oz (250 g) fillet of smoked trout

8 oz (250 g) smoked salmon

1/2 gala melon

1/2 bunch dill

4 fl oz (125 ml) mayonnaise of the best quality

1 tbsp sherry

1 lime

Preparation time: approx. 25 minutes
Per serving: approx. 313 cals/1311 kj

1 Cut the fish into bite sized pieces. Halve the gala melon and deseed. Using a scoop, scoop out small balls. Wash and dry the dill and chop finely.

2 Mix together the mayonnaise, sherry and dill. Arrange the fish on side plates and add the gala melon balls. Finally, pour over the sauce.

3 Thinly slice the lime. Garnish the salad with a little dill and lime slices. Toast or French stick make an ideal accompaniment.

Peach Rocket Salad

1lb (500 g) mixed lettuce leaves

3 1/2 (100 g) oz rocket salad leaves

5 oz (150 g) Parma ham

8 oz (250 g) tinned peaches

6 tbsp olive oil

3 tbsp vinegar

salt

pepper

cashew nuts for decoration

Preparation time: approx. 20 minutes
Per serving: approx. 274 cals/1150 kj

1 Wash and dry the lettuce and rip into bite sized pieces. Wash and dry the rocket salad.

2 Cut the Parma ham into thin long strips. Drain the peaches using a colander and slice into very thin strips.

3 Mix the oil and vinegar and season with salt and pepper. Transfer all salad ingredients into a bowl and add the dressing. Leave for five minutes to steep.

4 Arrange on glass plates and garnish with the cashew nuts.

Feel like an alternative salad dressing? Just season 3 1/2 oz yoghurt with a generous helping of curry powder, salt and pepper and add a little juice from the peaches.

Potato Salad

1lb (400 g) small potatoes

10 oz (300 g) round tinned carrots

12 boiled quail's eggs from the glass

5 oz (150 g) courgettes

3 1/2 oz (100 g) black olives, stoned

3 1/2 oz (100 g) pickled onions

3 tbsp olive oil

3 tbsp balsamico vinegar

1 tsp mustard

pepper

3 1/2 oz (100 g) lamb's lettuce

Preparation time: approx. 30 minutes
Per serving: approx. 287 cals/1205 kj

1 Peel the potatoes and simmer for 15 minutes in salted water. Drain the carrots and quail's eggs. Peel and slice the quail's eggs.

2 Wash the courgette and use a scoop to scoop out small balls. Drain the olives and pickled onions.

3 Slice the olives. Mix together the olive oil, the vinegar and the mustard. Season well with salt and pepper.

4 Wash and dry the lamb's lettuce and arrange on plates. Slice the cooked potatoes and arrange all ingredients on the lettuce leaves. Your dish is ready to serve.

If you have to be especially quick about it you could always use ready peeled and cooked potatoes. Fry them in a pan using walnut oil. They make a perfect base for all salads.

Soups and Stews

How to convert the best ideas into a delicious meal – and be as quick as lightning about it! Soups are not only very fast and simple to make, but they taste absolutely delicious, are healthy and fill that gap. Thanks to our recipes each spoonful will leave you dying for more!

Shrimp Avocado Soup

1 lemon

3 ripe avocado pears

2 pints (1 l) fish stock

7 oz (200 g) cooked shrimps

salt

freshly milled pepper

chilli powder

3 oz (80 g) crème fraîche

Preparation time: approx. 10 minutes
Per serving: approx. 292 cals/1228 kj

1 Squeeze the lemon. Peel the avocado pears, halve them, remove the stones and cut into bite sized pieces. Finally pour the lemon juice over the avocado pieces.

2 Blend with a hand-mixer. Heat the fish stock and add the mousse and shrimps.

3 Leave to simmer for approximately five minutes. Season with salt, pepper and the chilli powder. Garnish each plate with a spoonful of crème fraîche and serve.

Clear Flower Broth

1lb (400 g) tinned clear ox-tail soup

2 carrots

1 parsnip

1/2 avocado pear

salt

pepper

3 tbsp sherry

1 bunch parsley

Preparation time: approx. 25 minutes
Per serving: approx. 304 cals/1276 kj

1 Pour the oxtail soup into a pot and heat gently. Wash, peel and slice the carrots.

2 Peel the parsnip, halve and slice it. Peel the avocado pear, halve it, remove the stone and slice, too.

3 Take a cutter in the form of a flower and cut little flowers out of the slices. Add the carrot and parsnip flowers to the soup and leave to steep for 8 minutes. Season with salt, pepper and the sherry.

4 Shortly before serving, add the avocado flowers. Wash, dry and finely chop the parsley and sprinkle over the soup. Serve with savoury cheese sticks.

Greek Chicken Stew

1 grilled chicken (approx. 2 lb/1 kg)

2 onions

2 cloves of garlic

2 tbsp olive oil

2 pints (1 l) chicken stock

4 tbsp lemon juice

1 sprig of thyme

7 oz (200 g) artichoke hearts

salt

pepper

3 1/2 oz (100 g) sour cream

Preparation time: approx. 30 minutes
Per serving: approx. 413 cals/1734 kj

1 De-bone and skin the chicken. Peel and dice the onions.

2 Peel the cloves of garlic. Heat the oil and add the onions and meat. Crush the garlic and add as well.

3 After about 4 minutes add the chicken stock and lemon juice. Wash, dry and finely chop the thyme.

4 Drain the artichoke hearts and cut into small pieces. Then add them together with the thyme to the chicken stock. Season with salt and pepper.

5 Leave to simmer on a low heat for about 8 minutes. Slowly add the sour cream. Transfer the soup onto plates and serve.

Just the ticket for a quick evening snack: this is the ideal follow up dish if you have roast chicken left over from the day before.

Pasta Seafood Soup

10 oz (300 g) green fettuccine

salt

1 lb (400 g) frozen, mixed seafood

2 onions

3 tbsp olive oil

2 cloves of garlic

pepper

2 pints (1 l) fish stock

2 tbsp tomato purée

1 bunch tarragon

Preparation time: approx. 40 minutes
Per serving: approx. 394 cals/1655 kj

1 Cook the pasta in slightly salted water for about 20 minutes or for as long as it says on the packet.

2 Wash and dry the seafood. Peel and dice the onions. Heat the oil in a pot and gently cook the onions. Add the seafood.

3 Peel, crush and add the cloves of garlic. Season well with salt and pepper. After about 5 minutes slowly add the fish stock.

4 Simmer gently for about 10 minutes on a low heat. Add the tomato purée. Drain the cooked pasta, hold it under running cold water for a second and add to the soup.

5 Wash and dry the tarragon. Pluck the leaves from the sprigs. Serve the soup and garnish with the tarragon leaves.

Do you have some left-over pasta in your refrigerator from last night? This recipe is an ideal way of using those leftovers.

Cream of Mackerel Soup

3/4 pint (375 ml) Asian soup stock

7 fl oz (200 ml) light beer

3 1/2 oz (100 g) single cream

4 egg yolks

1/2 bunch watercress

7 oz (200 g) smoked peppered mackerel fillet

salt

pepper

Preparation time: approx. 20 minutes
Per serving: approx. 345 cals/1452 kj

1 Heat the Asian stock and the beer in a pot. Leave to boil for approximately 15 minutes. Mix together the cream and the egg yolks.

2 Take the pot off the flame and leave to cool a little before you stir in the egg and single cream mixture to thicken the soup. Wash, dry and coarsely chop the watercress.

3 Slice the smoked pepper mackerel fillet and add to the soup. Leave to steep for about 4 minutes. Season with salt and pepper. A fresh French stick makes an ideal accompaniment.

Hot Thai Vegetable Soup

2 pints (1 l) Asian soup stock

8 oz (250 g) pickled pumpkin

7 oz (200 g) frozen peas and carrots

3 1/2 oz (100 g) baby corn (tinned or out of a jar)

3 1/2 oz (100 g) pickled onions

salt

pepper

1 tbsp ground curry

3 tbsp desiccated coconut

Preparation time: approx. 20 minutes
Per serving: approx. 266 cals/1120 kj

1 Pour the stock into a pot and place it on the heat. Add the pickled pumpkin including the liquid, peas and carrots.

2 Drain both the baby corn and pickled onions using a colander before adding them to the soup. Season with salt, pepper and curry powder.

3 Leave to simmer for about 10 minutes on a low flame. Serve in soup bowls and garnish with the desiccated coconut.

Snacks and Finger Food

It does not matter if you serve them between meals or for a cosy evening with a nice group of guests: if you lack time, snacks and finger foods are simple to prepare. Serve them quickly and concentrate on your guests: the appetizers are already waiting for you.

Tongue Ragout Vol-Au-Vent

1 onion

7 oz (200 g) chanterelle

5 oz (150 g) cold tongue meat

3 tbsp butter

1 oz (30 g) flour

1/2 pint (300 ml) milk

7 fl oz (200 ml) single cream

5 oz (150 g) frozen peas

1 fl oz (2 cl) port

salt

pepper

lime juice

1 bunch coriander

8 mini vol-au-vents

Preparation time: approx. 25 minutes
Per serving: approx. 656 cals/2755 kj

1 Peel and dice the onions. Wash and dice the chanterelle.

2 Slice the cold tongue meat. Melt the butter in a frying pan and gently cook the onion, chanterelle and cold tongue meat for about 4 minutes.

3 Sprinkle in the flour, stirring constantly. Add the milk and single cream. Then add the peas and season with salt, pepper, lime juice and port.

4 Wash and dry the coriander. Pluck the leaves and add them to the mixture. Fill the vol-au-vents with the ragout and garnish with coriander leaves. Serve.

Savoury Toppings

7 oz (200 g) courgettes

1 apple

1 lb (500 g) curd cheese

7 tbsp olive oil

1 clove of garlic

4 sprigs coriander

salt and pepper

16 small wholemeal French stick slices

2 oz (50 g) sunflower seeds

3 1/2 oz (100 g) cashew nuts

3 tbsp balsamico vinegar

2 tbsp cream cheese

1 red pepper

8 basil leaves

Preparation time: approx. 20 minutes
Per serving: approx. 476 cals/1999 kj

1 Clean the courgettes and apple and grate them coarsely. Mix the curd cheese with 4 tablespoons of olive oil and add crushed garlic. Wash and chop the coriander and add to the cheese together with the courgettes and apple.

2 Season with salt and pepper. Put 8 wholemeal French stick slices onto your work surface and spread the mixture on. Roast the sunflower seeds in a frying pan without oil and sprinkle over the bread.

3 Using a hand-mixer, blend the cashew nuts together with the rest of the olive oil until you have a smooth mixture. Fold in the cream cheese and vinegar.

4 Wash the red pepper properly. Halve and deseed before chopping it into very small pieces. Wash and dry the basil. Cut into strips and fold into the mixture together with the red pepper.

5 Spread the mousse onto the other 8 wholemeal French stick slices. Garnish with herbs. Serve together with the bread.

Mini Pizza Parade

10 oz (300 g) pizza dough

handful flour to work the dough

3 1/2 oz (100 g) tomato purée

5 oz (150 g) spring onion, cut into rings

3 1/2 oz (100 g) blue veined cheese

2 tbsp pumpkin seeds, chopped

3 1/2 oz (100 g) tomatoes, sliced

3 1/2 oz (100 g) smoked eel fillet sliced

1 tbsp capers

1 red onion, cut into rings

3 1/2 oz (100 g) tinned sardines

1/4 bunch basil, cut into strips

3 1/2 oz (100 g) black olives, sliced

1/2 oz (10 g) anchovy fillet

3 1/2 oz (100 g) tinned artichokes, sliced

2 oz (50 g) tinned tuna

3 oz (80 g) mozzarella

Italian herbs

Preparation time: approx. 40 minutes
Per serving: approx. 643 cals/2665 kj

1 Sprinkle a generous helping of flour over your work surface. Then roll out the pizza dough. Using a small round cutter, cut out five small pizzas of about 4 inches in diameter.

2 Spread the tomato purée on the pizzas. Put the blue veined cheese on the first pizza and sprinkle with the spring onion rings and chopped pumpkin seeds.

3 Cover the surface of pizza number two with the tomato slices, eel fillets and drained capers. Put the onion rings, sardines and basil on top of the third pizza.

4 Cover the fourth pizza with the olive slices and anchovies. On pizza number five put the artichokes, tuna and mozzarella. Finally, sprinkle the herbs over all the pizzas and transfer in the centre of the oven for 15 minutes.

Be creative!
Lse other ingredients to put or. your pizzas.
Have a look in your larder or refrigerator.
Do not shy away from using urccnventional
combinations for a chcnge!

Omelette Bites

8 eggs

4 tbsp milk

1 bunch parsley

salt

freshly milled black pepper

paprika

1 oz (20 g) butter

1 onion

3 1/2 oz (100 g) Parma ham

2 tbsp oil

10 oz (300 g) frozen spinach leaves

3 cloves of garlic

5 tomatoes

7 oz (200 g) bean sprouts

Preparation time: approx. 30 minutes
Per serving: approx. 402 cals/1690 kj

1 Pour the eggs and milk into a bowl. Wash and dry the parsley. Cut into strips and mix together with the milk and eggs.

2 Season with salt, freshly milled black pepper and paprika. Melt the butter in a frying pan and cook as many omelettes as possible with the mixture.

3 Peel and dice the onions. Cut the Parma ham into strips. Heat the oil and gently cook the onions and ham. Add the spinach. Peel and crush the cloves of garlic and add to the frying pan.

4 Wash, dry and slice the tomatoes and add to the frying pan. Wash and drain the bean sprouts using a colander and also add to the frying pan.

5 When hot, season everything with a good deal of salt, freshly milled black pepper and paprika. Place the vegetables on the omelettes and fold Arrange on plates and garnish with some herbs.

Gone are the days when you only came across bean sprouts in Asian food. If you grow the sprouts yourself, they should sprout in at least five or six days. Otherwise, they are tasty enough out of a tin, too.

VARIATION

Spread mustard sauce, cocktail sauce and ketchup on the omelettes and stack on top of one another. Cut into triangles and arrange on a bed of lettuce leaves.

Salmon Rolls

7 oz (200 g) smoked salmon

1 tsp horseradish

2 tbsp lemon juice

1 onion

2 oz (60 g) mayonnaise

8 oz (250 g) puff pastry

paprika

dill for decoration

Preparation time: approx. 15 minutes
Per serving: approx. 527 cals/2213 kj

1 Cut the salmon into strips and mix together with the horseradish and lemon juice. Peel and dice the onion.

2 Add the diced onions and mayonnaise to the salmon. Preheat the oven to gas mark 6 (400° F or 200° C). Roll out the puff pastry and cut out a circle of about 8 inches in diameter.

3 Spread the salmon mixture over the pastry, then cut it into sixteen segments. Roll up each segment starting at the broad end and sprinkle with paprika.

4 Put the rolls onto a baking tray covered with greaseproof paper and transfer in the centre of the oven. Bake for approximately 15 minutes. Garnisheverything with dill.

Cheese Fricos

1 lb (500 g) grated mild cheddar

2 tbsp crumbled cornflakes

1 fl oz (2 cl) kirsch

1/2 tsp caraway seeds

1/2 tsp ground cardamom

1/4 tsp ground clove

1/4 tsp ground aniseed

1 egg

salt and pepper

3 1/2 oz (100 g) breadcrumbs

oil for deep frying

a choice of dips

Preparation time: approx. 20 minutes
Per serving: approx. 1726 cals/3049 kj

1 Mix together the cheese, cornflakes and kirsch and divide into three portions. Season the first portion with the caraway seeds, the second with the ground cardamom and the last with the ground clove and aniseed.

2 Form balls out of the mixture. Put the egg in a bowl, give it a quick whisk with a fork and season with salt and pepper. Dip the balls into the beaten egg and then roll in the breadcrumbs.

3 Heat the oil in a chip pan and fry the balls until they reach a golden brown colour. Serve the cheese fricos with dips of your choice.

Quick Meals from Oven and Pan

It does not matter which of our recipes for the frying pan you try: you can be sure that at the end of the day you will have a quick and tasty meal on your plate. Or let the oven do the work for you while you throw on the glad rags for your guests or simply relax after a long day at work. Oven recipes are very simple to prepare, always turn out well and leave plenty of scope for culinary creativity.

Mushroom Pineapple Chicken

13 oz (400 g) mushrooms

butter to grease the baking dish

4 chicken breast fillets (4 oz/125 g each)

7 oz (200 g) tinned sliced pineapple

1/2 stock cube

1 tsp cornflour

10 fl oz (300 ml) single cream

black pepper

4 tbsp sliced almonds

Preparation time: approx. 30 minutes
Per serving: approx. 514 cals/2152 kj

1 Preheat the oven to gas mark 6 (400° F or 200° C). Wash and slice the mushrooms. Grease an oven-proof dish with butter and cover with the mushroom slices.

2 Wash and dry the chicken breast fillets. Drain the pineapple slices, cut into pieces and place on top of the chicken fillets.

3 Dissolve the stock cube in hot water and mix with the cream and cornflour. Season with black pepper and pour into the oven-proof dish. Sprinkle sliced almonds over the casserole, put it in the centre of the oven and bake for about half an hour.

Salmon Gratin with Spinach

10 oz (300 g) frozen spinach

1 lb (500 g) fillet of salmon

butter to grease the oven-proof dish

1/2 stock cube

1 tsp cornflour

black pepper

1 pint (500 ml) single cream

3 tbsp pine kernels

Preparation time: approx. 35 minutes
Per serving: approx. 605 cals/2533 kj

1 Preheat the oven to gas mark 6 (400° F or 200° C). Defrost the spinach following the instructions on the packet. Wash and dry the fillet of salmon.

2 Grease the oven-proof dish and line with the spinach. Add the salmon pieces. Dissolve the stock cube in a little hot water and mix together with the single cream and cornflour. Season with pepper.

3 Pour the sauce over the salmon fillets. Sprinkle the pine kernels over the gratin, place the oven-proof dish in the centre of the oven and bake for approximately 25 minutes. Serve with rice or green fettuccine.

For those who like it especially tasty, we would suggest grating some fresh parmesan cheese into the sauce.

Chickpea Casserole

13 oz (400 g) tinned chickpeas

1 bunch spring onions

7 oz (200 g) peeled tomatoes

4 tbsp olive oil

5 oz (150 g) chorizo (spicy Spanish sausage)

1/2 bunch parsley

3 sprigs thyme

6 eggs

salt

pepper

1/2 pint (250 ml) milk

butter to grease the oven-proof dish

Preparation time: approx. 30 minutes
Per serving: approx. 547 cals/2299 kj

1 Drain the chickpeas using a colander. Wash, dry and slice the spring onions. Slice the tomatoes.

2 Heat the oil in frying a pan and gently cook the chickpeas together with the spring onions and tomatoes. Dice the chorizo and add to the frying pan.

3 Wash, dry and finely chop the herbs. Put into a bowl, add the eggs and give the mixture a good whisk with a fork. Season with salt and pepper. Add the milk and mix well. Preheat the oven to gas mark 4 (350° F or 180° C).

4 Grease an oven-proof dish with butter and fill with the mixture from the frying pan. Pour over the egg mixture and put in the centre of the oven. Bake for 15 minutes. Before serving, decorate the dish with herbs.

The egg mixture thickens during baking and binds all the ingredients together to a compact casserole. You can add single cream, crème fraîche or sour cream to the milk for extra finesse.

Turkey à la Mexicana

4 turkey escalopes (6 oz/180 g each)

salt

pepper

paprika

3 tbsp olive oil

10 oz (280 g) tinned Mexican vegetable mix

2 tbsp chilli sauce

1 packet wraps

Preparation time: approx. 15 minutes
Per serving: approx. 588 cals/2471 kj

1 Wash, dry and slice the meat into thin strips and season with salt, pepper and paprika. Heat the oil in a frying pan and brown the meat for approximately 3 minutes on all sides.

2 Drain the vegetables using a colander. Add them to the meat and pour in the chilli sauce. Simmer everything for about 4 minutes on a low heat.

3 Prepare the wraps following the instructions on the packet and spread on the work surface.

4 Fill the wraps with the vegetable mixture, roll up and serve.

Fishcakes with Tarragon

2 tbsp clarified butter

8 fish cakes (ready-made)

2 egg yolks

1 tsp Dijon mustard

grated rind of 1/2 lemon (untreated)

2 tsp lemon juice

1/4 pint (125 ml) sunflower oil

salt

pepper

1/4 bunch tarragon

Preparation time: approx. 15 minutes
Per serving: approx. 440 cals/1850 kj

1 Melt the clarified butter in a frying pan and fry the fishcakes for approximately 8 minutes. In the meantime, transfer the egg yolks, mustard and grated lemon rind to a bowl and mix together.

2 Add the oil drop by drop, whisking fiercely the whole time until the mixture begins to thicken. Finally, season with salt and pepper.

3 Wash, dry and finely chop the tarragon and add to the mayonnaise.

4 Arrange the fishcakes on plates. Serve with the mayonnaise. An ideal accompaniment are fried potatoes.

Mexican Bean Casserole

13 oz (400 g) tinned red kidney beans

13 oz (400 g) tinned Mexican corn mix

butter to grease the oven-proof dish

13 oz (400 g) corned beef

3 eggs

1/2 pint (250 ml) single cream

1/2 pint (250 ml) red wine

1 tbsp paprika paste

salt

pepper

paprika

Preparation time: approx. 50 minutes
Per serving: approx. 547 cals/2299 kj

1 Drain the beans and corn mix using a colander. Grease an oven-proof dish with the butter.

2 Layer the corned beef, corn and beans in the oven-proof dish. Mix together the eggs, single cream, red wine and paprika paste in a bowl. Season with salt, pepper and paprika.

3 Pour the egg mixture over the filling and place in the centre of the oven. Bake for approximately 40 minutes.

Beans, sweetcorn and chillies are at the core of the Tex-Mex cuisine. Kidney beans are red, shaped like kidneys and are usually used for chilli con carne. They are quite sweet and have a floury consistency when cooked.

Baked Black Salsify

1 lb (500 g) tinned black salsify

3 shallots

3 tbsp walnut oil

7 oz (200 g) deep frozen broccoli Romanesco

salt and pepper

freshly grated nutmeg

7 fl oz (200 ml) chicken stock

butter to grease the oven-proof dish

2 tbsp chopped hazelnuts

8 oz (250 g) Roquefort

Preparation time: approx. 20 minutes
Per serving: approx. 370 cals/1555 kj

1 Drain the black salsify using a colander. Peel and dice the shallots. Heat the oil in a frying pan and cook the shallots gently.

2 Add the broccoli Romanesco and black salsify and season with salt, pepper and freshly grated nutmeg. Slowly add the chicken stock and leave to simmer on a low heat for about 5 minutes.

3 Preheat the oven to gas mark 4 (350° F or 180° C). Grease an oven-proof dish with the butter. Pour the mixture into the dish and sprinkle with hazelnuts.

4 Crumble the Roquefort with a fork and spread over the casserole. Place in the centre iof the oven and bake for approximately 10 minutes.

Sauerkraut-Gratin

9 oz (280 g) sauerkraut

8 oz (250 g) smoked pork chop

4 fl oz (125 ml) beef stock

salt

1 tsp caraway seeds

butter to grease the oven-proof dish

ground black pepper

7 oz (200 g) brie cheese

Preparation time: approx. 20 minutes
Per serving: approx. 373 cals/1567 kj

1 Drain the sauerkraut using a colander. Cut the smoked pork chop into thin strips. Mix the sauerkraut together with the stock and meat.

2 Season with the caraway seeds, salt and pepper. Preheat the oven to gas mark 4 (350° F or 180° C). Grease the oven-proof dish with the butter and fill with the mixture.

3 Slice the cheese and spread as a lattice over the casserole. Place the dish in the centre of the oven and bake for approximately 10 minutes.

Brussels Sprouts and Tomato Casserole

1 lb (500 g) frozen Brussels sprouts

4 fl oz (125 ml) chicken stock

10 oz (300 g) tomatoes

salt

pepper

1/4 tsp dried oregano

freshly grated nutmeg

butter to grease the oven-proof dish

5 oz (150 g) Parma ham

3 1/2 oz (100 g) grated mild cheddar

Preparation time: approx. 30 minutes
Per serving: approx. 318 cals/1338 kj

1 Blanch the Brussels sprouts in the chicken stock for approximately 3 minutes. Pop the tomatoes into boiling water, hold under running cold water and skin them. Slice the tomatoes and add to the chicken stock.

2 Season well with salt, pepper, oregano and the freshly grated nutmeg. Grease an oven-proof dish with the butter. Preheat the oven to gas mark 6 (400° F or 200° C). Transfer the mixture into the casserole.

3 Cut the Parma ham into thin strips and spread together with the cheese over the casserole. Put in the centre of the oven and bake for approximately 20 minutes.

Red Cabbage Minced Meat Sandwich

1 round Turkish bread

7 oz (200 g) feta cheese

1 lb (500 g) tinned red cabbage

2 tbsp olive oil

1 lb (500 g) minced onion sausage

salt

pepper

Preparation time: approx. 25 minutes
Per serving: approx. 922/3875 kj

1 Cut the Turkish bread into quarters. Slice so as to make a pocket. Be careful not to separate the top and bottom. Dice the feta cheese.

2 Drain the red cabbage using a colander. Heat the oil in a frying pan and brown the minced onion sausage. Preheat the oven to gas mark 4 (350° F or 180° C).

3 Fill the Turkish bread with the minced onion sausage, feta cheese and red cabbage. Season well with freshly milled black pepper. Place the Turkish bread in the centre of the oven and bake for approximately 15 minutes.

Ratatouille Chilli

1 onion

1 clove of garlic

2 tbsp oil

13 oz (400 g) frozen ratatouille mix

1 lb (500 g) minced beef

2 tbsp tomato purée

salt

pepper

chilli powder

1 tsp provencale herbs

13 fl oz (375 ml) beef stock

1 bunch parsley

Preparation time: approx. 20 minutes
Per serving: approx. 723 cals/3038 kj

1 Peel and dice the onion. Peel and finely chop the clove of garlic, too. Heat the oil in a frying pan and brown the minced beef together with the onion, ratatouille mix and the garlic.

2 Add the tomato purée and season with salt, pepper, chilli powder and provencale herbs. After approximately 6 minutes add the beef stock and simmer for a further 5 minutes.

3 Wash, dry and finely chop the parsley. Arrange the chilli on plates, decorate with the parsley and serve.

You can feed a great number of hungry mouths with a good sized pot of chilli. And in case it does not get finished, you can easily heat it up again the following day.

Meat and Vegetable Fry

1 bread roll

1 lb (500 g) minced meat

1 onion

1 egg

salt and pepper

3 tbsp peanut oil

1 lb (500 g) frozen Chinese vegetables

1/2 pint (250 ml) chicken stock

ground ginger

ground mustard

4 tbsp soy sauce

Preparation time: approx. 15 minutes
Per serving: approx. 532 cals/2235 kj

1 Soak the bread in water and squeeze well. Rip the bread roll into small bits and mix together with the minced meat. Add the egg, season with salt and pepper and mix well. Wet your hands and form the mixture into small balls.

2 Brown the minced meat balls in the hot peanut oil. Cook on a low heat for approximately 8 minutes. Remove the balls and keep warm.

3 Put the frozen Chinese vegetables in the frying pan with the oil from the meat balls, brown gently and then add the chicken stock. Leave on a low flame to simmer for approximately 5 minutes.

4 Season with salt, pepper, ginger powder, mustard powder and soy sauce. Arrange the meat balls together with the vegetables on plates and serve. White rice makes for an ideal accompaniment for this dish.

Gammon with Leek

4 thick gammon slices (7 oz/200 g each)

2 oz (50 g) flour

1 egg

3 1/2 oz (100 g) breadcrumbs

2 tbsp sunflower oil

1 1/4 lb (600 g) frozen creamed leeks

1 fl oz (2 cl) aniseed liqueur

freshly grated nutmeg

2 tomatoes

4 slices pumpernickel

herbs for decoration

Preparation time: approx. 25 minutes
Per serving: approx. 487 cals/2045 kj

1 Cover both sides of the gammon with flour, dip into the beaten egg and then turn over in the breadcrumbs. Heat the oil in a frying pan and fry the gammon slices for approximately 4 minutes.

2 Place the frozen creamed leeks and aniseed liqueur into a pot and prepare, following the instructions on the packet. Season with freshly grated nutmeg.

3 Wash and quarter the tomatoes. Then halve each quarter again. Arrange the slices of pumpernickel on plates and cover with the gammon slices.

4 Spread the creamed leek onto the gammon slices and cover with the tomato. Finally, decorate with herbs.

Rissole Julienne

2 1/2 oz (75 g) bacon

1/4 stock cube

1 tsp cornflour

1 lb (500 g) minced beef

freshly milled black pepper

2 tbsp sunflower oil

1 large carrot

1 green pepper

2 oz (60 g) mushrooms

3/4 oz (20 g) butter

1/2 stock cube

3 fl oz (80 ml) cider

4 fl oz (125 ml) single cream

Preparation time: approx. 30 minutes
Per serving: approx. 225 cals/942 kj

1 Dice the bacon. Dissolve the stock cube and cornflour in 4 fl oz water. Add the minced meat and bacon, season with freshly milled black pepper and form into largish balls.

2 Heat the oil in a frying pan and brown the rissoles from all sides. Then remove from the frying pan, place on a kitchen towel to get rid of any extra oil and keep warm.

3 Wash and peel the carrot. Cut into thin strips. Wash the green pepper, halve lengthways, deseed and cut into thin strips. Wash and slice the mushrooms.

4 Melt the butter in a frying pan and gently cook the carrot, green pepper and mushroom strips for approximately 5 minutes. Crumble the stock cube into the frying pan.

5 Add the cider and single cream. Leave to cook on a low heat until the mixture is starting to thicken. Potato salad or mashed potatoes make an ideal accompaniment for this dish.

VARIATION

Add approximately 7 oz Emmental or cheddar cheese cubes to the meat mixture. Try snow peas instead of green peppers for the sauce.

For those who like it a little hotter, we recommend adding a finely chopped chilli and two crushed cloves of garlic to the meat mixture for extra taste.

Veal Cutlets in Basil

4 veal cutlets (7 oz/200 g each)

4 tbsp olive oil

salt

pepper

4 tbsp ready-made basil pesto

5 oz (150 g) yoghurt

1 tbsp lemon juice

2 spring onions

Preparation time: approx. 15 minutes
Per serving: approx. 438 cals/1842 kj

1 Wash and dry the meat. Heat the oil in a frying pan and brown the cutlets for about 8 minutes. Season with salt and pepper.

2 In the meantime, mix together the yoghurt, pesto and lemon juice and season with salt and pepper. Wash, dry and finely chop the spring onions.

3 Mix the chopped spring onions into the pesto mixture. Arrange the meat on plates, add the creamy mixture and serve with a French stick.

Smoked Sausage Bites

1 1/2 lbs (800 g) smoked sausage

3 tbsp flour

5 eggs

4 tbsp breadcrumbs

3 tbsp oil

13 oz (400 g) beetroot balls from the glass

4 gherkins

1 tbsp capers

2 onions

3 tbsp butter

Preparation time: approx. 20 minutes
Per serving: approx. 625 cals/2625 kj

1 Cut the sausage into somewhat thicker slices and turn over in flour. Beat one egg with a fork and dunk the sausage slices into it.

2 Then cover with breadcrumbs, making sure they stick well to the sausage slices. Heat the oil in a frying pan and fry the sausage slices.

3 Drain the beetroot balls, gherkins and capers. Peel the onion and cut it into rings. Melt the butter and fry four eggs.

4 Arrange the sausage slices on the plates, add the fried eggs and the condiments and serve.

Meat and Fish Dishes

Good things come to those who wait – this is certainly not true for our meat and fish recipes. They are quick and easy to cook and a real pleasure to eat. Moreover, frozen foods often make for an ideal accompaniment. Well, now there is no more excuse. Get to it...

Spicy Rump Steaks

4 rump steaks (7 oz/200 g each)

salt

pepper

4 tbsp olive

oil

10 oz (280 g) lychees

3 1/2 fl oz (100 ml) Asian stock

3 1/2 fl oz (100 ml) dry sherry

1 tbsp chilli paste

7 oz (200 g) five-

minute-rice

3 1/2 oz (100 g) sour cream

Preparation time: approx. 20 minutes
Per serving: approx. 901 cals/3786 kj

1 Wash, dry and season the meat with salt and pepper. Heat the olive oil in a frying pan and brown the meat on both sides.

2 Add the lychees and their juice together with the Asian stock and sherry. Stir in the chilli paste and season with salt and pepper. Leave to simmer on a low flame for approximately 5 minutes.

3 Cook the rice following the instructions on the packet. Remove the meat from the frying pan and keep warm.

4 Bring the stock to boil and stir in the sour cream. Arrange the steaks and rice on plates and pour over the sauce. Your dish is ready to serve.

Lychees, the fruit of an Asian hardwood tree, have a delicate sour taste that is reminiscent of nutmeg or roses. This makes them an ideal accompaniment for both meat and poultry.

Gipsy Fish

3 pretzels

4 fish fillets (7 oz/200g each)

2 tbsp chilli sauce

1 tbsp paprika paste

salt

pepper

2 tbsp flour

1 egg

4 tbsp clarified butter

1 1/2 lb (800 g) pasta salad

Preparation time: approx. 20 minutes
Per serving: approx. 742 cals/3116 kj

1 Remove the salt from the pretzels and chop finely. Wash and dry the fish.

2 Mix together the chilli sauce and paprika paste and season with salt and pepper. Spread the mixture over the fish fillets, then turn them over in flour. Beat the egg and dip the fish into it.

3 Cover with breadcrumbs, making sure they stick to the fish fillets. Melt the clarified butter in a frying pan and fry the fish from all sides.

4 Arrange the fish fillets on plates. Pasta salad makes an ideal accompaniment.

Lamb with Onions

12 lamb cutlets

salt

pepper

1 clove of garlic

3 tbsp peanut oil

10 oz (300 g) Italian pickled onions

2 tbsp butter

3 1/2 oz (100 g) Italian herbs

2 tbsp sugar

3 tbsp yoghurt

Preparation time: approx. 30 minutes
Per serving: approx. 638 cals/2682 kj

1 Wash, dry and season the cutlets with pepper and salt. Peel the clove of garlic and crush, then spread over the meat. Leave to steep for a little while.

2 Heat the peanut oil in a frying pan and brown the meat. Drain the Italian pickled onions before you halve them. Melt the butter and gently cook the onions and herbs together.

3 Sprinkle in the sugar and leave to caramelise for 10 minutes. With about a minute left add the yoghurt.

4 Arrange the cutlets on plates. Decorate with the onion in their sauce. A loaf of ciabatta makes an ideal accompaniment.

Fillet of Pork with Beans

10 oz (280 g) tinned white beans with greens

1 tbsp chilli sauce

1 tbsp red wine vinegar

1 tbsp seasoning for venison

1 tsp mulled wine seasoning

2 fillets of pork (13 1/2 oz/400 g each)

salt

pepper

oil to fry the meat in

Preparation time: approx. 20 minutes
Per serving: approx. 520 cals/2184 kj

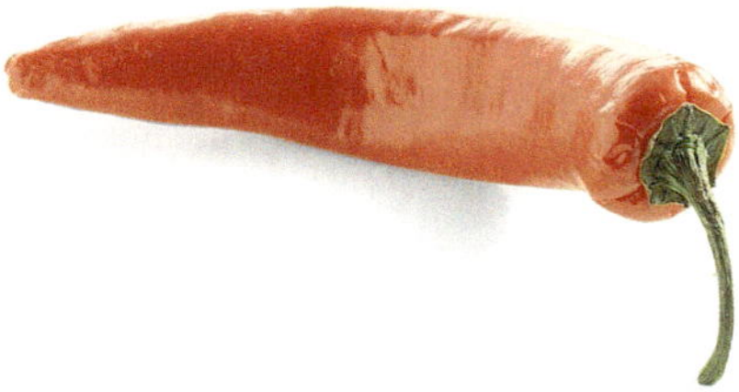

1 Drain the beans using a colander. Take a bowl and mix the beans together with the chilli sauce, red wine vinegar, venison seasoning and mulled wine seasoning.

2 Blend the mixture to a mousse with a hand-mixer. Wash, dry and cut a pocket into the meat.

3 Stuff the mixture into the pockets. Use wooden toothpicks to seal the whole. Season with salt and pepper.

4 Heat the oil in a frying pan and brown the meat. Before serving, slice the meat and arrange on plates with mashed potatoes.

The savoury bean mixture also goes well with hare or venison.

Rosemary Escalopes

1 sprig rosemary

2 tbsp olive oil

6 oz (180 g) cream cheese with paprika

salt

pepper

4 pork escalopes

8 slices Parma ham

1 lemon

Preparation time: approx. 20 minutes
Per serving: approx. 587 cals/2467 kj

1 Wash and dry the rosemary. Pluck the leaves off the sprigs and chop them finely. Heat the olive oil in a frying pan and gently fry the rosemary.

2 Add the cream cheese and season with salt and pepper. Wash and dry the meat. Season with salt and pepper. Spread the cream cheese mixture on the escalopes, cover with two slices of Parma ham and twist into a roll.

3 Reheat the rosemary oil and brown the escalopes on all sides. Arrange on plates, sprinkle with lemon juice and serve. Potato salad goes really well with this dish.

Braised Goose Joint

2 frozen goose joints

salt

pepper

4 tbsp sesame oil

7 oz (200 g) greens

1 pint (500 ml) chicken stock

1/2 pint (250 ml) red wine

7 oz (200 g) fruit and nut mix

ground aniseed

ground coriander

7 oz (200 g) sour cream

Preparation time: approx. 1 hour 20 minutes
Per serving: approx. 740 cals/3110 kj

1 Wash and dry the joints. Season with salt and pepper. Heat the sesame oil in a roasting tin and roast the joints from all sides. Preheat the oven to gas mark 4 (350° F or 180° C). Clean and wash the greens.

2 Add the chicken stock and red wine. Chop the greens and add together with the fruit and nut mix. Season with salt, pepper, ground aniseed and ground coriander.

3 Place in the centre of the oven and bake for approximately 60 minutes. Then take out the joints and keep them warm.

4 Bring the stock to the boil, blend and add the sour cream to give it the last touch. Baked potatoes make for an ideal accompaniment.

Dover Sole in Ginger Cream

8 frozen fillets of Dover sole

3 tbsp herb butter

salt

lemon juice

1 onion

1 clove of garlic

2 tbsp butter

1 small piece ginger

pepper

1/2 pint (250 ml) rice wine

2 tbsp soy sauce

3 1/2 fl oz (100 ml) crème fraîche

herbs for decoration

Preparation time: approx. 20 minutes
Per serving: approx. 396 cals/1666 kj

1 Wash and dry the Dover sole fillets. Melt the herb butter in a frying pan and sauté the fish. Season with salt and lemon juice.

2 Peel and dice the onion. Peel and crush the clove of garlic. Melt the butter in a frying pan and sauté the onions and garlic.

3 Peel the ginger, grate and add to the onions. Season with salt and pepper. Add the rice wine and soy sauce. Simmer on a gentle heat for approximately 5 minutes.

4 Stir in the crème fraîche. Arrange the Dover sole fillets and sauce on plates and decorate with herbs. Green fettuccine taste great with this dish.

Would you like a glass of wine with your fish? The ideal wine as an accompaniment to fish is a dry, quite light, not too flowery but slightly acidic wine. We recommend a German grey burgundy from Baden-Wurttemberg, a Riesling from the Alsace, an Italian Pinot Grigio or a French Pouilly Fumé.

Caribbean Liver

8 oz (250 g) frozen exotic fruits

4 slices pig's liver

(5 oz/140 g each)

7 oz (200 g) crème fraîche

3 tbsp mango chutney

1 1/2 fl oz (4 cl) white rum

4 tbsp flour

4 tbsp peanut oil

salt, cayenne pepper

1/4 bunch coriander

1/4 bunch watercress

3 1/2 fl oz (100 ml) vegetable stock

1 fl oz (2 cl) sherry

Preparation time: approx. 20 minutes
Per serving: approx. 724 cals/3042 kj

1 Mix together the defrosted exotic fruits, crème fraîche, mango chutney and white rum. Leave to steep for approximately 5 minutes.

2 Wash and dry the liver. Dip it in the flour. Heat the oil in a frying pan and fry the liver. Season with salt and pepper. Wash, dry and finely chop the herbs.

3 Remove the liver from the frying pan and keep warm. Add the vegetable stock to the frying pan and bring to the boil. Add the herbs and sherry.

4 Arrange the liver, fruit and sauce on plates. Pasta with a tomato sauce makes for an ideal accompaniment for this dish.

Fillet of Plaice on Potato Fritters

12 frozen potato fritters

8 fillets of plaice (3 1/2 oz/ 100 g each)

1 tsp lemon juice

salt

pepper

2 oz (50 g) clarified butter

2 red onions

1 big apple

2 oz (50 g) chopped bacon

Preparation time: approx. 15 minutes
Per serving: approx. 583 cals/2448 kj

1 Prepare the potato fritters following the instructions on the packet. Wash and dry the fish and sprinkle the lemon juice over it. Season with salt and pepper.

2 Melt the clarified butter in a frying pan and fry the fillets of plaice. Peel and cut the onions into rings. Peel, halve, core and quarter the apple. Then slice the quarters thinly.

3 Place the chopped bacon into a frying pan and wait a little while until the fat has melted. Then add the onions and apple slices.

4 Season with salt and pepper. Place three potato fritters on each plate. Arrange the plaice on top and sprinkle with the onions and apples.

Breast of Duck with Dip

2 breasts of duck with skin

2 tbsp walnut oil

salt

pepper

paprika

butter to grease the oven-proof dish

1/2 pint (250 ml) red wine

6 tbsp ready made Cumberland sauce

1/4 pint (125 ml) port

1 oz (30 g) currants

4 tbsp finely chopped walnuts

Preparation time: approx. 30 minutes
Per serving: approx. 749 cals/3147 kj

1 Preheat the oven to gas mark 4 (350° F or 180° C). Wash and dry the meat. Score the skin with a sharp knife in a diagonal lattice.

2 Heat the walnut oil in a frying pan and brown the meat. First fry the skin to a golden colour and season with salt, pepper and paprika. Then turn the meat just once. Grease an oven-proof dish with the butter.

3 Place the meat in the oven-proof dish, skin face-up. Add the red wine and place in the centre of the oven. Bake for approximately 10 minutes.

4 Heat the Cumberland sauce and port, add the currants and simmer for 3 to 4 minutes. Roast the walnuts in a pan. Slice the meat and arrange it on plates. Pour on the sauce and sprinkle with the walnuts. Potato crisps make an ideal accompaniment.

Part of a housewife's inventory: always cook the breast of duck in the oven after you have fried it. This way the outside becomes lovely and brown without burning and the inside always stays pink and juicy.

Hake Rolled in Bacon

4 fillets of frozen hake

lemon juice

8 rashers bacon

salt

pepper

3 tbsp clarified butter

1/2 pint (250 ml) fish stock

1 fl oz (2 cl) rum

5 tbsp mango chutney

2 tbsp thick-cut marmalade

dill or lemon balm and lemon pepper for decoration

Preparation time: approx. 30 minutes
Per serving: approx. 406 cals/1706 kj

1 Wash and dry the defrosted hake. Sprinkle with the lemon juice and place the bacon on top. Season with salt and pepper. Roll up the hake fillets and secure with a wooden toothpick.

2 Melt the clarified butter in a frying pan and brown the fish rolls on all sides for approximately 6 minutes. Remove the fish from the frying pan and keep warm.

3 Add the fish stock to the frying pan and pour in the rum. Leave to simmer gently on a low heat for approximately 4 minutes.

4 Bring the stock to the boil and stir in the mango chutney and thick-cut marmalade. Season with salt and pepper. Place the fish into the frying pan again.

5 Arrange the hake on plates and pour the sauce over it. Sprinkle with a bit of lemon pepper and decorate with the lemon balm or the dill. Wild rice makes a tasty accompaniment to this dish.

If you can buy a whole fish you will notice that the difference between the fresh and the frozen product is not a great one: while fresh fish is put on ice straight after the catch to cope with long transportation times, the frozen fish is frozen on the trawler itself.

Salmon in Orange Butter

4 middle cuts of salmon (7 oz/200 g each)

lemon juice

3 tbsp olive oil

salt

pepper

1/2 pint (250 ml) orange juice

3 tbsp pernod

1 orange, unwaxed

2 tbsp butter

dill for decoration

Preparation time: approx. 20 minutes
Per serving: approx. 634 cals/2663 kj

1 Wash and dry the salmon and sprinkle with the lemon juice. Heat the olive oil in a frying pan and brown the salmon for approximately 4 minutes on each side. Season with salt and pepper.

2 Heat the orange juice and pernod in a smaller pot. Wash the orange and scrape off the peel. Add the butter and the peel to the orange juice and let it steep for approximately 4 minutes.

3 Shortly before it is ready, season with salt and pepper. Arrange the salmon on the plates, pour the sauce over and decorate with the dill. Pasta makes an ideal accompaniment.

Add a little butter to the fried salmon, wait for it to start melting before basting the salmon with it. This improves the salmon's flavour.

Leipzig Delight

4 fillet steaks (5 oz/150 g each)

3 tbsp clarified butter

salt

pepper

1 1/4 lbs (600 g) frozen mixed vegetables

2 oz (50 g) dried morel

3 1/2 oz (100 g) cooked and peeled king prawns

1/4 pint (125 ml) beef stock

1/4 pint (125 ml) wheat beer

5 oz (150 g) sour cream

Preparation time: approx. 30 minutes
Per serving: approx. 866 cals/3499 kj

1 Wash and dry the meat. Melt the clarified butter in a frying pan and brown the meat for approximately 5 minutes on all sides. Season with salt and pepper.

2 Drain the vegetables using a colander. Soak the morel in water for some 10 minutes. Remove the meat from the frying pan and keep warm.

3 Add the drained morel, vegetables and king prawns to the frying pan and cook gently. After approximately 5 minutes, add the beef stock and wheat beer. Season with salt and pepper.

4 Leave everything to steep for about 4 minutes. Just before it is ready, stir in the sour cream. Arrange the meat and vegetables on plates. You might want to try croquettes as an accompaniment to this dish.

A perfectly cooked steak is not rocket science if you follow these instructions: never beat or pierce the meat. Brown the meat under a high flame for about 1 minute, then reduce the heat a little. When you have cooked the steaks, wrap them in aluminium foil and leave to rest for a while. This ensures that they stay nice and juicy.

Vegetarian Meals

Healthy and quick to prepare: if you are not in the mood for meat, we have a nice selection of the finest vegetarian ideas that will turn out great without a lot of preparation. Just take a look in your refrigerator or larder. We bet that you can throw together a lovely vegetarian recipe with the ingredients you find in there.

Artichokes with Creamy Sauce

13 oz (400 g) artichoke hearts

1 fl oz (2 cl) sherry

1/4 pint (150 ml) vegetable stock

1/2 pint (250 ml) ready-made Béarnaise sauce

salt

pepper

3 tbsp garlic croûtons

tarragon for decoration

Preparation time: approx. 20 minutes
Per serving: approx. 258 cals/1084 kj

1 Drain the artichoke hearts. Heat the vegetable stock and the sherry. Add the artichoke hearts and simmer for about 4 minutes.

2 Remove the artichoke hearts and place into a colander. Add the Béarnaise sauce to the vegetable stock and simmer for a while until it is well mixed. Season everything with salt and pepper.

3 Arrange the artichoke hearts on plates, pour over the sauce and garnish with the garlic croutons and tarragon.

Artichokes are North African thistles
for connoisseurs.
If fresh, the fleshy flower heads
are cooked in slightly salted water
with a touch of lemon juice for about thirty minutes.
You eat them by plucking off the leaves one by one
and dunking them in sauce
before sucking out the flesh.

Couscous with Pumpkin

1 lb (500 g) pre-cooked couscous

1/2 pint (250 ml) vegetable stock

7 oz (200 g) pickled pumpkin out of a glass

2 small fennel bulbs

2 tbsp chopped pumpkin seeds

1 tbsp fennel seeds

salt

pepper

1 pinch harissa

fennel leaves for decoration

Preparation time: approx. 20 minutes
Per serving: approx. 504 cals/2118 kj

1 Cook the couscous following the instructions on the packet. Heat the vegetable stock. Drain the pumpkin using a colander and add to the stock.

2 Wash and finely slice the fennel and add to the vegetable stock. Leave to simmer on a low heat for approximately 5 minutes.

3 Mix together the pumpkin seeds and fennel seeds and roast in a frying pan without oil or butter. Add the couscous to the stock and season with salt, pepper and the harissa.

4 Arrange everything on plates and sprinkle with the pumpkin and fennel seeds. Garnish with the fennel leaves.

Gnocchi in Red Wine Sauce

13 oz (400 g) gnocchi from the packet

13 oz (400 g) goat's cheese

3 tbsp olive oil

13 oz (400 g) chopped tomatoes

salt

pepper

1 tsp dried thyme

1/4 pint (125 ml) red wine

herbs for decoration

Preparation time: approx. 20 minutes
Per serving: approx. 439 cals/1846 kj

1 Cook the gnocchi following the instructions on the packet. Dice the goat's cheese. Heat the olive oil in a frying pan and cook the goat's cheese and chopped tomatoes.

2 Season everything with salt, pepper and thyme. After approximately 2 minutes, add the red wine and leave to simmer on a low flame for about 4 to 5 minutes.

3 Drain the gnocchi using a colander and arrange together with the sauce on plates. Decorate with herbs and serve.

Large Mushrooms with Dip

13 oz (400 g) large mushrooms

2 cloves of garlic

2 tbsp olive oil

salt

freshly milled black pepper

7 oz (200 g) salad cream

4 tsp sweet mustard

1 tbsp crème fraîche

1 bunch dill

sugar

1 French stick with herbs

Preparation time: approx. 20 minutes
Per serving: approx. 435 cals/1828 kj

1 Clean the large mushrooms and cut into thick slices. Peel and crush the cloves of garlic.

2 Heat the olive oil in a frying pan and gently cook the mushrooms together with the garlic. Season with salt and pepper.

3 In the meantime, mix together the salad cream, sweet mustard and crème fraîche. Wash and dry the dill and pluck off the leaves. Stir into the dip.

4 Season with salt, pepper and a little bit of sugar. Arrange the mushrooms on the plates and add the dip. Decorate with the dill. Serve with the French stick.

You add a special provencale touch by frying the mushrooms and then adding 1/2 pint of red wine. Leave to simmer for 15 minutes

Arabian Spinach Purée

7 oz (200 g) onions

2 cloves of garlic

10 oz (300 g) frozen spinach leaves

1/2 bunch parsley

7 fl oz (200 ml) vegetable stock

5 tbsp black olives

3 tbsp olive oil

salt

pepper

cumin

cardamom powder

1 tbsp lemon juice

1 Turkish bread

Preparation time: approx. 20 minutes
Per serving: approx. 292 cals/1227 kj

1 Peel and dice the onions. Peel and finely chop the cloves of garlic. Defrost the spinach leaves following the instructions on the packet.

2 Wash, dry and finely chop the parsley. Heat the vegetable stock. Add the onions, garlic and the spinach and leave to simmer for approximately 5 minutes.

3 Drain the olives using a colander and cut into slices. Heat the olive oil in a frying pan and add the olive slices. Drain the spinach leaves and then add to the olives.

4 Season the spinach with salt, pepper, cumin, cardamom and lemon juice. Mix with a fork. Put the Turkish bread in the oven. When hot, slice open and stuff with the mixture.

This is a Moroccan dish and can be cooked in a lot of regional varieties. You can also use chard instead of spinach.

Sweets and Desserts

Being short of time does not mean you have to do without a sweet or dessert. You can prepare delicious bits and bobs that sweeten up your evening in less than quarter of an hour.

Tasty Tea Creme

1 1/2 tsp green tea leaves

1 1/2 fl oz (4 cl) dry vermouth

1 fl oz (2 cl) vodka

2 tbsp orange juice

2 tbsp lemon juice

7 oz (200 g) mascarpone

3 1/2 fl oz (100 ml) single cream

lemon balm for decoration

Preparation time: approx. 10 minutes (plus chilling time)
Per serving: approx. 362 cals/1522 kj

1 Prepare the tea with 7 fl oz of boiling water. After approximately 5 minutes strain through a sieve and leave to cool.

2 Mix with the dry vermouth, vodka, orange juice and lemon juice.

3 Stir in the mascarpone and single cream. Transfer into small dishes and leave to cool. Prior to serving decorate with the lemon balm.

You can also prepare this dish with a variety of other ingredients. For example, instead of green tea you might want to try herbal or aromatic teas.

Calvados Apples

10 oz (300 g) tinned calvados apples

10 oz (300 g) vanilla ice cream

7 fl oz (200 ml) single cream

sugar

cinnamon

lemon balm for decoration

Preparation time: approx. 10 minutes
Per serving: approx. 350 cals/1471 kj

1 Drain the calvados apples using a colander. Make sure you retain the juice.

2 Mix together the vanilla ice cream, the juice from the calvados apples and the single cream. Season with sugar and cinnamon.

3 Arrange the apples on plates and pour over the vanilla sauce. Garnish with the lemon balm and serve.

VARIATION

You must also try this dish with fresh exotic fruit such as figs or cumquats. The latter are dwarf oranges, the peel of which is untreated and edible.

Vanilla Raspberry Dessert

1 instant custard (for 1 pint milk)

1 pint (500 ml) milk

3 tbsp ricotta cheese

1 fl oz (2 cl) raspberry brandy

13 oz (400 g) frozen raspberries

chocolate sticks and lemon balm for decoration

Preparation time: approx. 15 minutes (plus chilling time)
Per serving: approx. 257 cals/1081 kj

1 Prepare the vanilla sauce following the instructions on the packet. Mix the ricotta, the raspberry brandy and the raspberries.

2 Transfer the vanilla sauce into four small dessert bowls and add the raspberry mixture.

3 Leave to cool in the refrigerator until firm. Then garnish with the chocolate sticks and lemon balm and serve.

Hot Ice Cream

4 frozen ice cream croissants

7 oz (200 g) fresh or frozen exotic fruit

2 fl oz (4 cl) rum

3 1/2 oz (100 g) natural yoghurt

3 1/2 oz (100 g) chopped walnuts

Preparation time: approx. 10 minutes
Per serving: approx. 611 cals/2569 kj

1 Prepare the croissants following the instructions on the packet. Wash, peel and cut the fresh fruit into bite sized pieces. Alternatively, defrost the frozen fruit. Sprinkle the rum on the fruit.

2 Mix the fruit with the natural yoghurt and heat in a pan.

3 Arrange the croissants on plates and add the fruit mixture. Sprinkle with the chopped walnuts and serve.

Tangerine Yoghurt

10 oz (300 g) tinned tangerines

3 tbsp peppermint syrup

2 tbsp lime juice

13 oz (400 g) natural yoghurt

vanilla sugar

1 bunch fresh mint

2 oz (50 g) preserved cocktail cherries

Preparation time: approx. 10 minutes
Per serving: approx. 207 cals/872 kj

1 Drain the tangerines and place in a bowl. Add the peppermint syrup, lime juice and yoghurt and mix well.

2 Sweeten with a little sugar. Transfer the tangerine yoghurt into a little dessert bowl.

3 Wash and dry the sprigs of mint. Pluck off the leaves and drain the cocktail cherries. Garnish the tangerine yoghurt with the mint leaves and cocktail cherries and serve.

You can make a lovely cool fitness drink in the summer if you add buttermilk to the tangerine yoghurt and blend thoroughly.